# Life Stories Journal

## Your Stories
## for Your Loved Ones

To purchase multiple copies or to request permissions,
contact the publisher at CJIGARLLC@gmail.com

Paperback: ISBN 979-8-68-770943-9

Published in the United States of America.

Journal copy written and design by Catie Chung.

# Welcome

This is a book I wish I could have shared with my dad when he was still alive. How's that for a bright and sunny start to what is supposed to be a bright and sunny book??

As a Registered Nurse and as a nursing professor, I have talked with thousands of people about how important their families are to them. Whether it's worry when one of your family is sick or going back to graduate school to create a better future for your family, we all want the best for our people.

The years pass so quickly!

We're busy...
But the busyness of life isn't what gives it meaning, is it?

Our stories are how we share treasured memories.

Our memories give life meaning.

This book is intended to help capture those treasured memories. Whether the memories are yours, or you work through this book with a loved one to preserve their memories, the process of working with this book can create another treasured memory for all involved.

# Welcome

My dad had beautiful cursive handwriting. I would have had him write out his stories or make notes in his handwriting to capture his writing as well as his stories.

Another really fun thing to do is tell a story from both of your perspectives – some of the most detailed memories I have of my dad are events that dad and I were at together and then talked about after they happened, when we got to laugh about how we each experienced the fun.

As far as we know, we only get to do this life once, and each of us has incredible unique experiences that need to be shared and preserved.

Whatever way you choose to use this Life Stories Journal, please relax and enjoy time well spent.
xoxo,
Catie

# How to Use this Book

Just use it!

If you or your loved one likes to draw, use the pages to draw out your responses to the prompts that resonate.

If your loved one likes to talk more than write, you can make notes in the journal and record their beautiful voice telling their story out loud.

Are little kids involved? Have them color the question pages they like the best and then answer those questions.

If a bunch of family is together, have everyone answer a question page!

Remember to jot down dates that are important and the dates that you're completing pages.

Dog-ear pages to come back to, underline or highlight questions you want answered... this book is meant to be used because stories are meant to be shared!

*"Tell me about a time when..."*

# This book is about
## my stories:

Is anyone working with you to help capture your stories? Who?

# Favorites...

What's your favorite color?
What's your favorite place?
How about your favorite smell?

Have those always been your favortes?

# More Favorites...

Food? Drink?
Song? Movie?
Book? Magazine?
Play? Opera?
Musical?
Painting? Artist?

# Your Stuff

Did you have a
favorite thing
you owned as a
kid?
Why was it your
favorite?

# Growing Up You

What did you think was funny
about your parents when you
were a kid?

Were there things your parents
did that you thought were really
great?

# Growing Up You

What music and
movies did you love
as a kid?
As a teen?
Did your parents
'approve'?

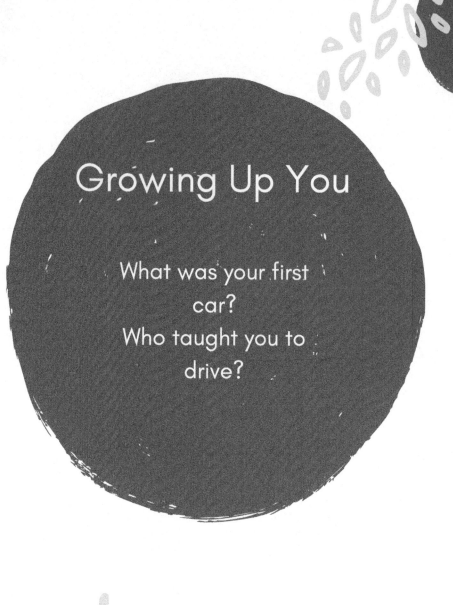

# Growing Up You

What was your first
car?
Who taught you to
drive?

# Best Friends

Who were your best
friends as a kid?
What did you do
together?
Are you still friends?

# School Days

Did you like school
as a kid? Why or
why not?
What was your
favorite subject in
school? What about
least favorite? Why?

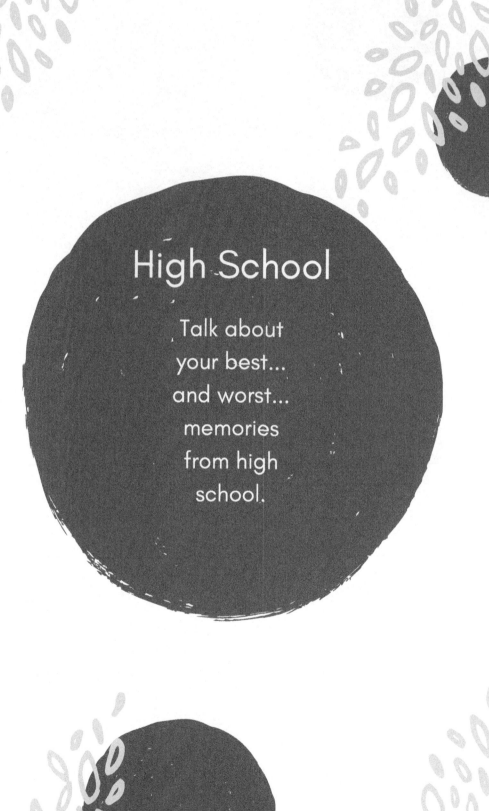

# High School

Talk about
your best...
and worst...
memories
from high
school.

# More School...

What were your schools like - public or private? Small or large? Close or far? Did you ride the bus? Your parents drop you off?

# Growing Up You

What did you like to
do – or have to do –
on the weekends
when you were
growing up? What
was your first job and
how old were you
when you got it?

# College or Military?

Did you go to
college? Enlist in
the military? Both?
Neither?
What were those
experiences like for
you?

# Around the House

Do you like to cook? Who taught you to cook? What is the recipe you like to make the most? Who do you like to cook for best?

# Family Time

What was your favorite
thing you did as a family
When you were a kid?
How about now? Do you
have a least favorite
thing you did as a family
when you were a kid?
Now?

# Chore Time!

What chores did you have to do when you were young? If you had siblings...did you argue with your siblings about chores?

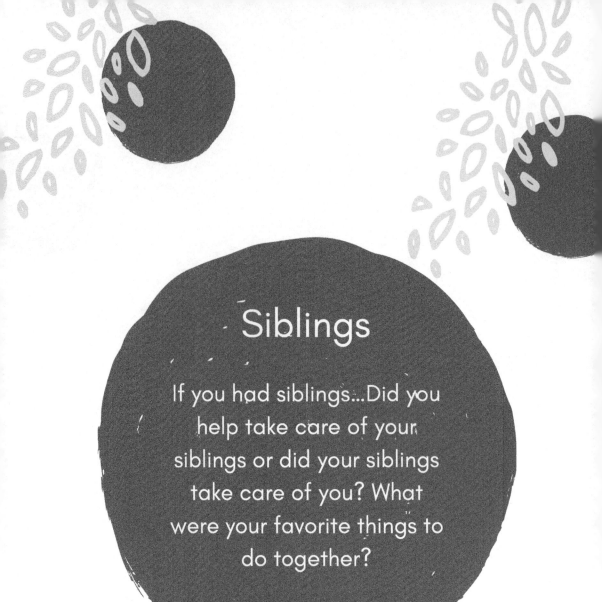

# Siblings

If you had siblings...Did you help take care of your siblings or did your siblings take care of you? What were your favorite things to do together?

# The Big Wide World

What was the world like when you were a little kid and teenager? What historical events do you remember? What were your experiences of those events? Did you think that stuff was important at the time?

# Just Wondering

What's the best
thing about your life
right now?
What has been your
favorite age so far?
Why?

# Seasons

What was your favorite
season when you were
growing up? Why... is it
about nature, or life events,
or food?
Is it still your favorite
season?

# Holidays

What was your favorite holiday
when you were growing up?
What parts of the holiday did
you love – the food, the
company, decorations, gifts?

# Holidays Through the Years

What was your favorite
holiday when you had
young children at home?
What is your favorite
holiday now?

# Holiday Food!

Lots of families have
special holiday food
traditions...what are yours?
Is there a holiday meal you
enjoy the most? Or do you
have one favorite dish?
Who makes it best?

# Holiday Gifts

Do you have a lifetime favorite gift you have received? What about lifetime favorite that you've given?

# What's your favorite place in the world?

Tell all about it...
why is it your
favorite? What dt
do you see, hear, &
smell there? Who
do you go with?

# Seasonal...

Do you have favorite
activities or places
for different
seasons?
Fall
Winter
Spring
Summer
?

# Vacations

Did you take vacations when you were a kid? What was the first real vacation you remember?
Who was with you, where did you go, what did you do?

# Vacations

What was the
best vacation you
have had so far?
Why?

# Your Better Half

How did you meet your
spouse? How did you
know s/he was 'the
one'? What is your
favorite memory about
your better half?

# Courting

How did you get to
know your better
half....what kind of
dates did you go on?
Did you write letters?
Did you have a long-
distance relationship?

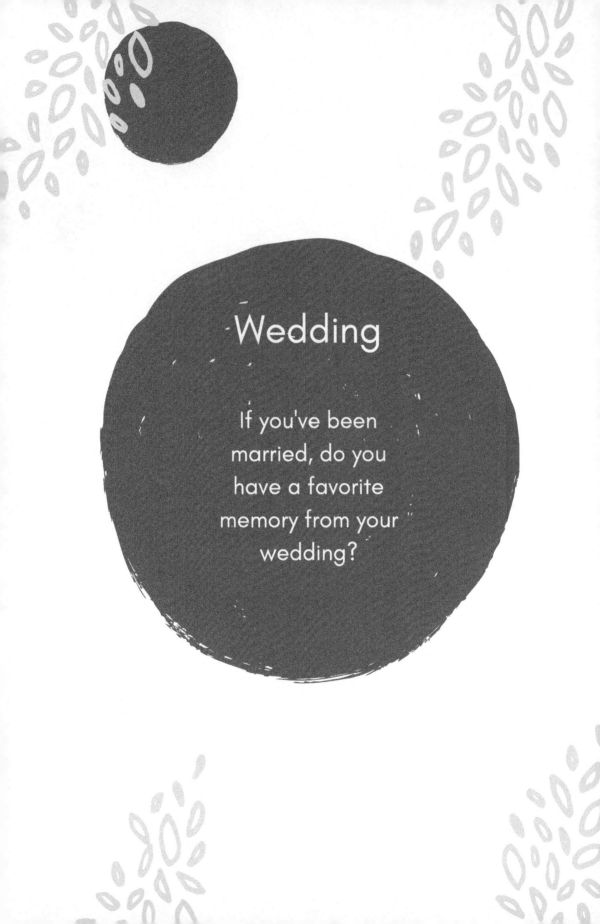

# Wedding

If you've been married, do you have a favorite memory from your wedding?

# Adulthood

When do you feel like
you "grew up" and
became an adult?
Was it a moment,
an event,
or an age?

# Adulthood

When you left home
how did things turn out
different than you
expected?

# Parenting

What was your
life like when
you had small
children?

# You as a Parent

What did you love the
most about being a
parent?
What was the hardest
part of being a parent?

# Eyes in the Back of your Head

What are some things you know about your kids that they believe they kept secret?

# Big Stuff: Religion

Did you go to a church-
temple-mosque (wherever!)
when you were a kid?
Regularly or not?
Did you and your parents talk
about religion?

# More about what's up there...

What do you believe now about religion? What about God or a Higher Power or other spiritual beings? Does that influence your daily life? How?

# Habits

Do you do the same thing when you first wake up each day? What habits do you have that you can't live without doing? Do you have any habits you'd rather not have?

# Best Friends

How many best
friends have you had
as a grown up? Who
are they? How did
you become best
friends?

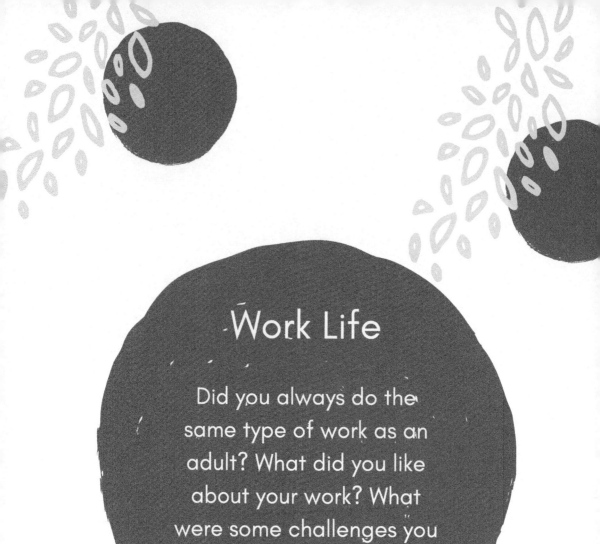

# Work Life

Did you always do the same type of work as an adult? What did you like about your work? What were some challenges you had during your career?

# Surprises

What has been
the biggest
surprise to you
about your
own life?

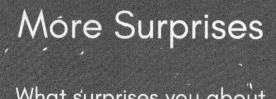

# More Surprises

What surprises you about
how your kids turned
out? What doesn't
surprise you about how
your kids turned out?

# Your Stuff Now

Do you have any
favorite things
now? What
means so much
to you about
them?

# Early Bird or Night Owl

What time of day do
you enjoy the most?

# Clothes

What are your favorite
outfits or styles of
clothing you've worn
through the years?
Include pictures too!

# When did your family come to the US?

Do you know their story?

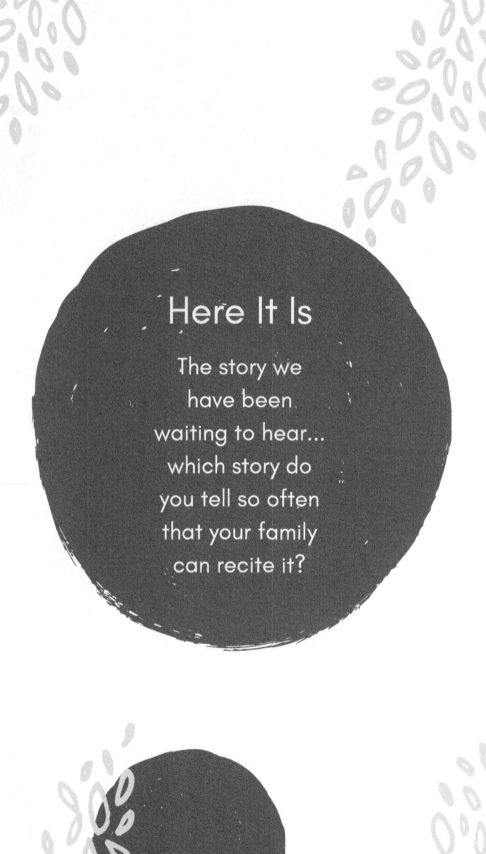

# Here It Is

The story we
have been
waiting to hear...
which story do
you tell so often
that your family
can recite it?

# Reflecting

Anything you wish
you started
sooner in life?
Anything you wish
you stopped
sooner in life?

# Making More Stories

Do you have
anything you want
to do on your
bucket list? When
are you going to
do that?

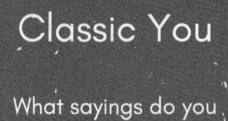

# Classic You

What sayings do you
say all the time?
Where did those
sayings come from –
what's the backstory?

# Advice

What is the
best advice you
want to share
with your loved
ones?

# Family History

What stories about your parents or grandparents should we keep passing down? Share the good, the bad, and the ugly!

# Anything else?

Can you think of
anything else you
want to tell your
loved ones?
Anything at all?

Keep making
memories
& sharing stories!

Made in the USA
Monee, IL
19 September 2023

43033699R00066